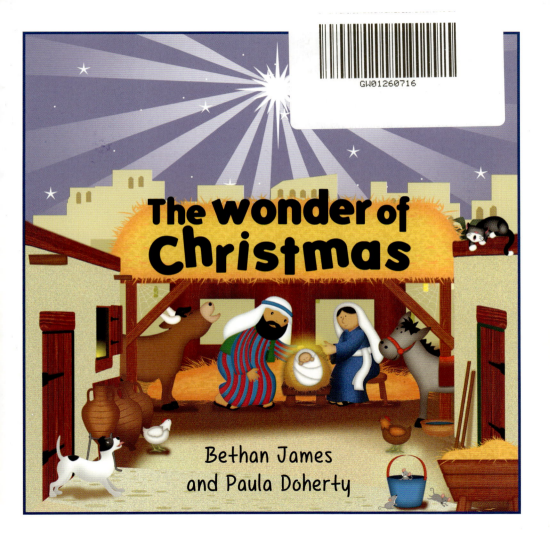

The angel Gabriel came to visit Mary. 'Don't be afraid,' he said – because Mary was afraid. She had never seen an angel before.

'I have wonderful news for you. God has chosen you to be the mother of Jesus, His Son; to take care of Him until He is ready to show the people of all the world how much God loves them.'

Mary didn't know what to say. She was not yet married. But she knew that she loved God. 'God is great and wonderful,' said Mary. 'I am ready to do this special thing for Him.'

Mary was engaged to be married to Joseph, a carpenter. When Mary found that she was pregnant and carrying God's Son, God told Joseph to take care of Mary and to marry her.

Joseph had to take Mary to Bethlehem. The Roman emperor wanted everyone to return to the place where their grandpa's grandpa's grandpa had been born. He wanted to count them so he could make them pay taxes!

Many other people had travelled to Bethlehem too, so when Mary and Joseph arrived they could not find a place to stay. There was not a single room at the inn.

Mary knew that very soon her baby would be born. She was far from home and needed somewhere to rest. She needed somewhere to put her baby when He was born.

Joseph found them a place where the animals sleep – a stable with straw on the floor and hay in the manger. It was not much of a home. It was not a palace fit for a baby king. But Mary was ready to stop and rest.

She felt the pains that meant that soon she would be a mother, holding her first-born baby in her arms.

That night, Mary's baby boy was born!

In the stillness of the night, Mary made a bed for Him in the manger and laid Him on the hay. They named Him Jesus, just as the angel Gabriel had told them.

All the animals in the town saw that something wonderful had happened.

The donkey brayed and the oxen mooed. The dog barked and the goat bleated. The cat meowed and the owl hooted.

It was not a silent night anymore! God's Son had come into the world and was born in Bethlehem. It was a wonderful thing!

That night, there were shepherds out in the fields watching over their sheep.

Suddenly the sky was filled with light! It was an angel!

'Do not be afraid,' he said. 'I bring you good news that will make you happier than you have ever been! God's Son, the one who has come to save you, has been born tonight in Bethlehem. He will bring peace to the world. You will know when you find the baby for He is lying in a manger.'

The shepherds could not believe what they were seeing – or what they had heard! But then the sky was filled with the light of thousands of angels, praising God and singing: 'Glory to God in the highest heaven – and peace to everyone who lives on earth!'

The shepherds could hear the sound of the wonderful music in their ears long after the angels had disappeared.

The shepherds ran to Bethlehem to see if they could find the baby the angel had told them about. They found Him lying in a manger and they praised God for Him. They told Mary and Joseph about the message of the angel – that Jesus, the baby in a manger, would bring peace to all the world.

Far away in the east, some wise men saw a new star appear in the night sky. What could it mean?

'A baby King has been born,' they decided.
'We must go to worship Him. We must pack special gifts for Him.'

So they travelled by night, following the star.

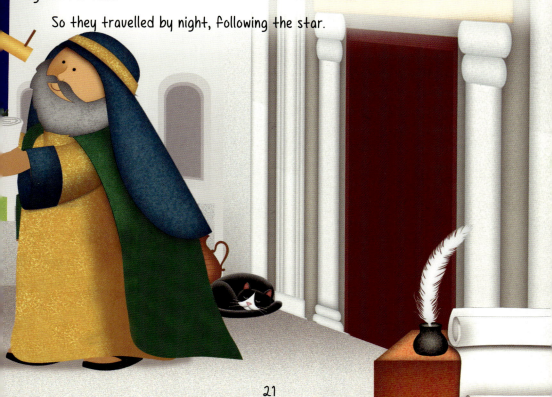

The star seemed to stop over a little house in Bethlehem. The wise men found Jesus with His mother, Mary. They knelt to worship the young King and to offer their gifts of gold, frankincense and myrrh.

As the visitors made their way home to their land in the east, Mary wondered at all she had seen. She knew that her little boy would grow up to change the world and bring peace to all the people on earth.

Copyright © 2017 Anno Domini Publishing
www.ad-publishing.com
Text copyright © 2017 Bethan James
Illustrations copyright © 2015 Paula Doherty
Editorial Director: Annette Reynolds
Art Director: Gerald Rogers
Design and pre-production: Doug Hewitt
All rights reserved
Printed in China
Published 2017 by CWR, Waverley Abbey House, Waverley Lane, Farnham, Surrey, GU9 8EP, UK
Registered Charity No. 294387. Registered Limited Company No. 1990308
For a list of National Distributors, visit www.cwr.org.uk/distributors